OUTRAGEOUS
PEACE

A Practical Path to
Real Peace—Even When
Nothing Else Has Worked

by
Beatty Carmichael

Published by Maran Ministries LLC

Outrageous Peace (vs 2.0—260309)
Author: Beatty Carmichael
Copyright © 2026 by Maran Holdings, LLC

This book is not intended to diagnose, treat, or replace professional medical, psychological, or therapeutic care. The author encourages readers to seek appropriate professional guidance when needed.

ISBN: 979-8-9890591-3-3

TABLE OF CONTENTS

DEDICATION

This book is dedicated to anyone who has quietly wondered why peace never seems to last.

To those who kept showing up, kept trying, and kept moving forward—even when something inside felt heavy or unsettled.

And to the people who walk beside them—friends, family members, and loved ones—who care deeply, even when they don't know how to help.

May this book be a gentle reminder that peace is not out of reach, and you were never broken for longing for it.

INTRODUCTION

Most people long for peace but never seem to find it—not because they aren't trying, but because they were never shown what actually creates peace. They've worked hard, stayed sincere, and done what they were told should help. And when peace still doesn't come, they quietly assume the problem must be them.

That assumption quietly costs them—confidence, energy, hope, and rest—as peace slips away under pressure.

By "pressure," I don't mean external pressure—deadlines, noise, conflict, or a demanding schedule. I mean internal pressure: the quiet strain that builds when something inside you stays unfinished. You can appear fine on the outside and still feel braced, tight, or mentally "on" inside. That's what this book is about.

What surprised me wasn't just that peace could return—but how often it did, across people whose struggles looked nothing alike.

Peace is the natural result of alignment—when what's been off inside you comes back into agreement with how life was designed to work, and the inner resistance finally stops.

Most people have some sense that life points

beyond itself—to a Creator, a higher power, or some greater intelligence behind it. People use different language for that. For simplicity, I'll use the word God here.

I was trained to think in terms of problem-solving—identify the cause, then apply the right remedy—so I assumed peace would come from the right intervention: therapy, better habits, or more discipline.

But over time, I began to notice a different pattern—that much of what people were experiencing wasn't malfunction, but misalignment with the way God designed life to work.

When alignment is restored, peace stops being something you chase—it begins showing up as a result of returning to God's design.

So, I began guiding people through a simple process: helping them identify what had been misaligned, face it honestly, and let it go.

And I began watching the same kinds of shifts repeat—anxiety lifting, depression loosening, relationship conflict softening, chronic pain often easing, even some addictions losing their grip. Not because life suddenly got easier, but because the internal strain underneath it finally lifted.

Over the years, I've personally walked more than 1,000 people through this process—not clinically, but in ordinary life with real people. In many of those moments, people reported an internal shift they could feel right away, like pressure releasing that they didn't realize they'd been carrying.

I'm not offering a diagnosis, and I'm not replacing medical or professional care. If you're under care, stay under care—this is meant to support what you're doing, not replace it.

I'm describing a pattern I've watched repeat—often quickly—when people address what's been quietly throwing their inner world out of alignment.

I can't promise the same experience for everyone, but it happens often enough to take seriously.

Most people have already tried everything they know to find peace. They think better. Breathe deeper. Pray harder. Stay positive. Push through. Some of it helps for a moment—but the pressure eventually returns.

The problem isn't effort.

Effort can compensate for a while, but it can't replace the design God built into your inner world.

One man told me his life had felt like carrying a backpack full of bricks. No matter how much he tried to relax, think positively, or pray his way out of it, the weight never lifted. But when he began living in alignment with the pattern you're about to learn, the shift was immediate. He said it felt like the weight dropped off in a single moment. The next morning, he woke up with a quiet mind, a light body, and a peace that felt more natural than anything he had ever forced.

That's what happens when peace stops being accidental and starts becoming the result of something real and dependable.

That "something real" is a pattern woven into the way God designed life to work, and it is already at work in your life right now. It is quiet and unseen, but not vague or mystical. Most people miss it because it operates beneath the surface. Once you recognize that pattern, peace stops feeling fragile—and your inner life starts to make sense.

Most of us have spent years managing symptoms instead of addressing roots. We try relaxation techniques, mindset tools, breathing exercises, positive affirmations, and spiritual practices. Some of these can be helpful, but they don't always reach the deeper causes behind the fear, tension, pain, or emotional heaviness we carry.

That's why peace can feel so hard to hold onto. Not because peace is weak, but because something underneath has been quietly pulling it away.

People say things like, "I keep fixing the same issues, but they always come back," or "No matter what I try, something still feels off." They're not imagining it. They're responding to a deeper reality they were never shown how to see.

Struggle isn't personal failure—it's often the result of something inside falling out of alignment.

Peace doesn't respond to effort.

Peace responds to alignment with how God designed life to work.

This book isn't meant to give you more techniques to try or more pressure to "do better." It's designed to guide you into an experience of peace—one that doesn't depend on your circumstances cooperating or your effort never slipping.

You don't need special knowledge to begin. You don't need to feel particularly hopeful. Wherever you are right now—curious, skeptical, exhausted, or simply tired of feeling the way you've been feeling—is enough.

You're standing at the edge of something most people were never taught to recognize.

As you read, you may begin to notice small shifts. A reaction that doesn't spike the way it used to. A heaviness that loosens its grip. A quietness that feels unfamiliar—but right. These moments aren't the finish line. They're signs that something real is already changing. Often the first sign is simple: your mind stops working so hard to hold everything together.

You're not stepping into a complicated spiritual system or a dense manual. You're stepping into a simple path—one that reveals what's been disrupting your peace and shows you how to address it.

Here's what to expect: you'll learn why peace

keeps slipping away, how to spot what's quietly keeping you braced inside, and a simple way to release that pressure so peace can start to feel normal again.

So, take a breath. You don't have to carry this alone anymore.

Let's begin.

— Chapter 1 —
When Peace Never Shows Up

Riley was only thirteen, but she carried herself like someone much older. Her shoulders curled inward. Her eyes stayed low. Even her breathing felt heavy. I had known her for years, and in all that time, I had never once seen her smile.

One afternoon, during a season when her family was coming apart, I sat with her in the kitchen and asked a simple question.

"Do you ever feel like you're carrying a backpack full of rocks?"

She nodded without looking up. "Yes. It feels heavy all the time."

There was no dramatic moment to point to. No single event that explained what she carried. No medical diagnosis that captured the weight she lived under. It was just a constant heaviness she had learned to accept as normal—like something she didn't remember ever putting down.

Fifteen minutes later, everything changed.

After a brief moment of prayer, Riley stood up, straightened her back, and drew in a deep breath—as if someone had lifted a hundred pounds off her body. Then she began to dance around the room. She twirled across the floor, humming to herself, smiling so widely that her mother froze as she watched in disbelief, tears starting to fill her eyes.

"Is it normal to feel physically lighter after this?" Riley asked, her face glowing.

"Yes," I told her. "That's exactly what peace can feel like."

Do you ever feel like you're carrying a weight you can't quite name—like something inside you never fully unclenches? Pressure in your chest. Tightness in your shoulders. Thoughts that won't settle. That sense of being braced inside—even when nothing is happening.

Maybe you wake up tired and go to bed tense. On the outside, you function. You do what needs to be done. You smile when you're supposed to. But inside, it feels like you're carrying something heavy that no one else can see. Over time, you may have told yourself, *This is just who I am*, or *This is just my life*.

If that sounds familiar, you're not alone.

And it's not your fault.

Most people live their entire lives without experiencing real peace—not the temporary calm that comes from a vacation or a quiet weekend, but the kind of peace that holds steady when life doesn't. People catch glimpses of it. A moment on a walk. A song that moves them. A deep breath that feels different. But it slips away the moment real life returns.

Peace feels fragile. Temporary. Unreliable.

Calm is often circumstantial—something you feel when life gets quiet. Peace is deeper. It's what you feel when the inside finally stops fighting you.

If you've never felt that kind of peace—or if you've only known it in rare flashes—there's a reason. And it has nothing to do with your willpower, your personality, your discipline, or your spiritual maturity.

Peace isn't missing because you're weak.

It's missing because no one ever showed you how life was designed to produce peace.

There is a pattern woven into how God built life—already operating beneath the surface.

It is quiet, consistent, and invisible—but dependable.

Whether you understand it or not, that design is already shaping what happens inside you.

For years, I watched people wrestle with anxiety, depression, chronic pain, heartbreak, addiction, and patterns they couldn't break. These weren't weak or unmotivated people. Many were thoughtful, capable, deeply sincere. They tried everything they were told to try—counseling, medication, lifestyle changes, stress reduction, positive thinking, spiritual practices.

Some of it helped for a while. But the heaviness always returned.

What I began noticing startled me. When the true root of their struggle was uncovered, a hidden peace flowed into places where pain had lived for years. People who had carried torment for decades suddenly felt light, clear, whole. Their circumstances didn't magically resolve. Their personalities didn't become perfect. But something deeper shifted—something inside finally let go.

I was trained to think in terms of what's wrong and how to fix it: identify symptoms, make a diagnosis, apply the right treatment.

If someone was still struggling, I assumed the solution was either incomplete or hadn't been applied long enough.

But again and again, I watched people who had done everything right remain stuck.

They didn't lack effort.

They lacked an understanding of the deeper order God built into life—and effort cannot substitute for that.

They weren't broken—they were misinformed.

They were trying to create peace from the outside in, using tools that were never designed to reach the source of their unrest. No one had shown them the deeper pattern woven into life that quietly governs the inner world. So they kept adjusting circumstances, habits, schedules, and coping strategies, hoping peace would finally stay. When it didn't, they assumed something must be wrong with them.

Nothing was wrong with them.

They were simply working against the design already shaping their lives—a design they had never been taught to recognize.

Think of driving a car with the alignment badly off. You can keep correcting, keep adjusting, keep white-knuckling your way down the road—and for a while, you stay in your lane. But it's exhausting. And the moment you relax your grip, the car drifts in the same direction again. The problem isn't the driver. The problem is deeper.

Peace works the same way. It returns when what's underneath comes back into right order.

It doesn't respond to effort. It responds when what has been off beneath the surface is finally set right.

When what's underneath is straightened out, peace stops being something you chase.

It becomes a steady underlying calm in your life. It doesn't erase pain, grief, or disappointment—but it keeps those things from owning you.

If peace has slipped through your fingers—if calm never holds, if heaviness feels familiar, if your mind won't settle and your heart won't rest—there is a reason. And once you see it, your life begins to make a new kind of sense.

That's what this book is about.

— Chapter 2 —
Why Peace Slips
Through Our Fingers

Most people want peace. They reach for it, pray for it, organize their lives around it, and cling to anything that promises even a moment of relief. And yet, no matter how sincere their efforts, peace keeps slipping through their fingers. It shows up briefly—a quiet morning, a relaxing weekend, a meaningful conversation—and then disappears the moment real life presses in again.

When this happens, most people assume the explanation is obvious. Life is stressful. Circumstances are difficult. Schedules are full. People are demanding. All of that plays a role—but none of it explains why peace is so fragile.

The real reason peace doesn't last is simpler—and far more relieving—than most people realize.

Peace doesn't come from effort. Peace settles when your inner world begins functioning the way God designed it to.

In other words, peace is not something you manufacture—it is something that appears when what has been out of alignment quietly returns to its proper place.

I saw this clearly with a young woman named Ashlyn.

For most of her life, Ashlyn lived under crippling anxiety and PTSD. Every morning she woke up terrified, convinced something terrible was about to happen. Her thoughts raced nonstop. Doctors prescribed heavy combinations of medication just to keep her functioning. Diagnoses shifted over time, but peace never arrived.

When I walked Ashlyn through the process you'll encounter later in this book, she didn't expect anything to change. She was exhausted and out of options. But as she moved through it, something shifted. The fear loosened. The heaviness lifted. The racing thoughts that had dominated her inner world for years went quiet—not because she forced them to stop, but because something underneath them released.

The next morning, she woke up without fear—something she had not experienced since childhood.

Nothing in her circumstances had changed. Her responsibilities were the same. What changed was something inside her finally settled back into alignment with the way God designed life to work.

Once alignment was restored, peace flowed in as though it had been waiting.

This is what most people misunderstand.

Peace doesn't come from rearranging the outside. It returns when the inside stops resisting what is true.

If you're skeptical of spiritual language, that's okay—keep reading for the pattern, and use whatever words feel honest to you.

Most people think peace is a feeling—calmness, quietness, relaxation. But **real peace is what remains when the inner pressure finally drops.**

If peace has never held for you, it is not because you failed. It's because no one ever showed you what peace actually responds to.

Once you begin to see that pattern, a different question naturally follows.

If peace returns when life comes back into alignment, how do you recognize when something inside has slipped out of alignment in the first place?

A Quiet Daily Practice

If something in these pages has stirred hope—or awakened a longing for deeper peace—I've created a short, guided daily peace prayer you can return to anytime.

It's a simple pause. A moment to breathe, release, and realign.

Some people use this prayer in the morning to begin the day grounded. Others return to it in the evening to let go of what they've been carrying. I hope you will find it helpful.

Access it now by scanning the code below or entering the URL.

OutrageousPeace.com/DailyPeace

— Chapter 3 —
Peace Responds
to Inner Conditions

Now, I want to help you recognize the signals that peace is being disrupted—not so you can manage them, but so you can understand what they reveal.

Misalignment usually doesn't show up with a siren to announce itself. It does not usually arrive with dramatic symptoms or obvious breakdowns. More often, it shows up quietly—in the way life begins to feel heavier than it should.

Most people recognize something is off not because they can name it, but because calm starts to require effort. Rest doesn't fully restore them. Their body feels subtly braced. Their mind never quite shuts off. They still function. They still show up. But everything takes more energy than it should—like you're carrying an invisible load all day long.

That strain is one of the clearest signs that something underneath is out of order. When something inside slips out of alignment, your mind and body begin compensating—working harder just to stay steady.

Over time, that compensation becomes so normal that most people stop noticing it. They assume the tension is simply part of life.

Not everything traces back to this kind of inner disruption. But lasting peace rarely stabilizes until something inside comes back into the order God intended.

And when peace starts thinning like that, the first thing most people notice is exactly what you've already felt: calm begins to require effort.

That effort is not a character flaw.

It's a signal that something is off—something inside hasn't fully settled yet.

Busy is a full calendar. Internal pressure is that feeling when you never quite relax—tightness, looping thoughts, irritability, that sense of being "on" even when nothing is happening.

Jackson understood this immediately when he finally put words to what he had been living with for years. On the outside, his life looked stable. On the inside, everything felt tight. Conversations escalated faster than he intended. Decisions felt heavier than they should. He told me, "It feels like everything takes effort."

Nothing in his life looked dramatic enough to justify the weight he carried. That's why he assumed the problem must be him.

But misalignment rarely looks dramatic.

In every system—mechanical, relational, physical—misalignment creates strain because things stop functioning the way they were designed.

The same pattern operates inside our inner world. When something inside slips out of alignment with the way God designed life to work, strain begins to appear long before the cause becomes obvious.

When alignment is lost, peace becomes fragile—easily disturbed and difficult to sustain.

Most people adapt to that strain without realizing what they're adapting to.

Adaptation is not the same as alignment.

It can keep you functioning, but it can't restore what's out of line.

Effort can compensate temporarily—but it cannot restore what's out of alignment.

As you read, you may notice familiar sensations—tension you've learned to live with, reactions that feel automatic, a low-grade pressure that never fully lifts.

Simply noticing these things is not failure. It is awareness. And awareness does not create problems—it reveals them.

Once something is seen clearly, it no longer has to be carried unconsciously—you stop hauling it around without realizing it.

And once you recognize that effort has only been compensating for misalignment, a deeper realization begins to emerge.

Trying harder was never going to resolve it.

That's not discouraging news. It's relief.

— Chapter 4 —
Why Trying Harder Never Worked

Most people assume peace disappears when life gets difficult. Stress increases. Pressure mounts. Responsibilities multiply. So, the solution feels obvious: manage life better. Try harder. Improve habits. Think more positively. Pray more sincerely.

For a moment, you feel steadier. Clearer. More in control. The edge softens. The noise quiets.

But the peace never seems to hold.

The moment you stop managing it, it slips away. Life presses in, and the calm you worked so hard to create dissolves. Before long, you're right back where you started—only now, more tired than before.

It's like leaving work without actually shutting things down. You can be at dinner, but part of you is still "at the office." And when you try to sleep, you toss—not because something is wrong with you, but because something inside is still running. Peace doesn't return until whatever's still running inside you finally settles and lets go.

If effort truly worked, peace would be common. A vacation would fix it. A new routine would fix it.

Enough insight would fix it. Enough discipline would fix it.

Yet many sincere, thoughtful, disciplined people remain exhausted.

That's because effort can only address what is visible. But what disrupts peace rarely begins on the surface—it usually starts deeper.

When peace is destabilized by something deeper, effort becomes compensation—a way of holding things together instead of addressing the cause.

Effort can maintain stability temporarily.

But it cannot restore what has slipped out of alignment beneath the surface.

You learn how to cope. You learn how to manage reactions. You learn how to stay functional despite the strain. From the outside, it can look like progress. Inside, it still feels tight.

One woman described it as holding her breath all day just to feel okay. The moment she relaxed, the strain rushed back in—like her system never trusted it was safe to let go.

Therapy can bring insight. Medication can reduce intensity. Lifestyle changes can improve focus and energy. Spiritual practices can bring comfort and perspective.

Many of these things are genuinely helpful.

But none of them were designed to restore what slipped out of alignment in the first place. They help you cope—they do not correct what is underneath.

So, peace comes and goes.

You feel better for a while.

Then something small happens.

Life applies pressure.

And the calm you worked so hard to maintain slips away again.

Over time, that pattern becomes confusing. People begin to question themselves—their character, their emotional capacity, their faith. The failure starts to feel personal, even when it isn't.

Trying harder never worked because effort was never the problem.

Trying harder cannot resolve what was never caused by weakness, laziness, or lack of discipline.

And once you see that, something important happens. Exhaustion softens. Self-blame loosens its grip. Hope comes back—quietly.

Because peace is not restored by managing strain.

Peace returns when what disrupted it is finally removed and life comes back into alignment with the way God designed it to work.

— Chapter 5 —
There's More Going On Beneath the Surface

By now, one thing may be getting difficult to ignore.

If peace isn't created by effort, discipline, or circumstances—and if trying harder never reached the root of the problem—then something deeper must be influencing what's happening inside you.

Most people were taught to look for answers only in what they can see.

If something hurts, they look at the body.

If something feels overwhelming, they look at thoughts or emotions.

If relationships feel strained, they look at communication and behavior.

All of that matters.

But it is not the whole picture—and never has been.

Whitney lived for more than twenty years with constant pain in her neck, back, and legs. Doctors explained it in structural terms—disc issues, nerve pain, sciatica. She adjusted how she moved, how she slept, how she worked. Over time, the pain stopped feeling like a problem to solve and started feeling like part of who she was.

What rarely came up was something else she carried—an unresolved weight from a past relationship that had never fully released—something she thought she had moved past, but never really set down. There was no dramatic story attached to it. No ongoing conflict. Just something unfinished that quietly stayed with her.

In her mind, these were separate realities. Pain was physical. The past was emotional.

They were not separate.

When she finally addressed what had remained unresolved, the change surprised her—not just physically, but internally—as if something she had been carrying for years had finally been set down.

This is where many people get stuck—not because they are unaware, but because they were never taught to look beyond the visible. They were never shown that what's unseen can still be very real.

Much of what shapes your inner life operates quietly beneath the surface—still real, even when it isn't obvious, because life continues responding to the way God designed it to work, even when we are unaware of it.

That's why you can be doing "fine"—and still snap at someone you love, lie awake with your mind racing, or feel tense in your body for no clear reason.

Most people don't question it. When they cannot point to a clear cause, they turn inward and assume the problem must be personal.

They weren't broken. They were simply missing part of the picture.

This idea isn't new. Ancient scripture describes the same reality.

In Psalm 32, the writer reflects on a time when he kept things buried inside instead of bringing them into the open. The pressure built until, as he described it, his strength felt drained and even ordinary days became exhausting—like strength fading away in the heat of summer.

Long before modern psychology described these patterns, people were already noticing that unresolved things inside us quietly affect the whole person—mind, body, and spirit.

Unseen influence doesn't need dramatic events to shape your life—it only requires time.

Once that possibility enters the picture, pieces that never quite fit begin to come together. The struggle starts to make sense. And the question shifts again—not toward effort or blame, but toward understanding.

If peace has been blocked by something deeper, it does not need to be forced.

It needs to be restored—which means whatever has been in the way must be removed.

And when what has been quietly interfering is finally addressed, peace does not need to be managed.

It returns naturally—when nothing is standing in the way.

— Chapter 6 —
How Peace Actually Returns

B y now, something subtle may already be starting to shift.

Not a dramatic breakthrough. Not a sudden answer. But a quieter change in how you begin to notice what's happening inside you. A softening of the belief that peace is something you must hold together by force—like realizing how tightly you've been holding on and finally loosening your grip.

That shift matters more than it may seem.

Most people assume peace returns the same way they think it was lost—through effort. If things feel heavy, they try harder. If calm slips away, they double down. And when peace still does not hold, they quietly decide the problem must be them.

Peace does not return through effort.

It returns when what has been weighing on you is finally allowed to lift and the strain underneath begins to release.

I have seen this happen more times than I can count.

Different stories. Different kinds of struggles.

But the pattern is remarkably consistent.

In Chapter 8, I'll walk you through a simple, spoken way to let the pressure go—not by force, but through honesty.

Bobby once described his life as feeling like he was carrying a backpack full of bricks—not just emotionally, but physically. He woke up tired, moved through his day braced, and went to bed with the same weight still pressing on him.

Nothing about his life looked dramatic. He was functioning. Responsible. Stable. But inside, everything felt heavy all the time.

As we talked, I did not ask him to fix himself or perform. I did not ask him to manage his reactions or try to be more disciplined. Instead, I helped him slow down long enough to notice what he had been carrying—and to face it honestly rather than continuing to compensate for it.

At one point, he paused, took a breath, and said quietly,

"It feels like the weight just lifted."

That was it.

The next morning, he woke up calm—not trying to be calm, just calm. His body felt relaxed. His thoughts were quiet. Peace felt like the foundation of his life instead of something he had to chase.

Peace does not require you to improve yourself.

It begins when truth is acknowledged instead of

avoided.

And that return to what is true begins with honesty.

Not harsh honesty. Not self-criticism. Simply truth—acknowledged without defense or explanation.

When something that has been carried quietly is finally brought into the open, the pressure it created begins to release.

You do not have to make peace happen.

You only have to let go of what blocks it and stop holding onto what no longer needs to be carried.

When that happens, the strain underneath begins to dissolve, and peace settles back into place.

— Chapter 7 —
What Blocks Peace

Now, let me name some of the most common things that keep peace from settling—not to create fear, but to remove the confusion about why effort alone hasn't worked.

Once you understand that peace can return without effort, a different question naturally arises.

If peace doesn't disappear because you failed, and doesn't return because you try harder, then what has been quietly standing in the way?

For most people, the answer is not dramatic. It is not extreme. And it is not something they chose on purpose.

Peace is usually blocked by ordinary human things that were never fully resolved—not crises or catastrophes, but experiences that were lived through, adapted to, and quietly carried forward.

What matters tends to surface on its own, without effort, when it is safe to do so.

Most of us never mark these moments as important. We keep moving. We do what is required. We adjust. Over time, the tension becomes familiar. It fades into the background of our daily lives—like background noise you eventually stop noticing.

Peace rarely vanishes all at once. It usually thins gradually.

And when it gradually thins, it is easy to miss what caused it.

This is especially true for those who are thoughtful, responsible, and sincerely trying to do things well.

We adapt rather than question.

We normalize strain rather than challenge it.

Over time, unrest starts to feel normal—even reasonable.

I have seen this clearly in people who did everything they knew to do. Rob and Lily were one of those couples. From the beginning, their relationship carried tension—not explosive conflict, but constant friction. Small arguments. An unsettled feeling that never quite went away.

Rob and Lily noticed it early enough that they began marriage counseling before they were even married.

They worked on communication. They learned tools. They tried to manage reactions.

And yet, peace never really settled.

The tension did not feel like failure. It felt familiar. This was not what they believed marriage should feel like—but it was what felt normal. So they adapted. They worked around it. They treated the unrest as something to manage rather than something to question—something to live with instead of something to explore.

Rob sensed it as a quiet instability, as if calm was always conditional. Lily carried it as an internal pressure she could not quite name. Neither could point to a single cause. But both lived with the same underlying sense that peace never fully arrived.

Nothing about their story points to irresponsibility or neglect. Quite the opposite. They were doing what capable, sincere people often do when peace does not come easily.

They worked on the symptoms.

What they had not yet recognized was that something underneath was still interfering with peace.

Peace was not absent because they lacked effort or because life was unusually hard.

It was being quietly obstructed by something unresolved—something still interfering with the way God designed peace to function in their lives.

This is how peace is most often blocked.

Not by obvious wrongdoing.

Not by dramatic trauma.

But by internal tension that became familiar enough to feel normal—so normal it stopped standing out.

Unresolved hurt.

Unfinished grief.

Old fear that never stood down.

Attachments that once made sense—but never fully released—a lingering pull that never quite let go.

Peace does not judge these places—but it can't settle while they remain unaddressed, still hidden in plain sight.

When people finally recognize what has been sitting beneath the surface, they often feel relief—not shame. They will say things like, "I didn't realize I was still carrying that," or "I thought I had moved on," or "That explains why peace never held."

And once you clearly see it, you no longer have to keep hauling it around unconsciously.

As you read, certain moments may come to mind without effort. A relationship. A season. A memory that still carries weight when you think about it. If that happens, simply notice. Do not push it away—and do not feel pressured to resolve it.

Peace does not demand speed.

Peace lifts when what is being held is finally allowed to let go.

And something is already making room for that release.

Peace is not going anywhere.

— Chapter 8 —
Stepping Into
Outrageous Peace

U p to this point, we've been talking about peace as something structural—something that follows alignment rather than effort. What we have not named clearly yet is where that alignment takes place within the life God designed.

To understand why peace lifts the way it does, we need to acknowledge something most people were never taught to see clearly: there is a part of human life where things are either in line—or they aren't. This is not about intensity or force. It's about coming back into alignment with what is already true within God's design for life.

At the center of this, as I understand it, is God—the source of life, truth, and order itself. We were designed with an inner capacity to recognize when something is true, when something is off, and when something needs to be set right. When our inner world moves back into agreement with what is true, peace follows naturally. When it does not, peace begins to thin.

You don't need to share all my language or background for what follows to make sense. If some spiritual terms feel unfamiliar, stay with the pattern itself.

What matters is simple: peace does not come from willpower. Peace comes when something inside returns to alignment with what is true and life-giving.

By peace, I don't mean a feeling—I mean **the absence of internal pressure.**

You're not being asked to relive your past or force anything to the surface—only to let whatever still carries pressure come into the open honestly. This step is simply about calling something what it is instead of continuing to carry it quietly. When that honesty happens, alignment begins to return—and peace begins to follow.

So, if something has felt heavy, unsettled, or un-resolved as you've read, simply noticing that is enough for now. You don't need certainty, perfect words, or even complete understanding. You are not being asked to perform. You are only being invited to respond honestly to what you already recognize inside.

The prayer that follows is simple, and I encour-age you to speak it out loud, even if it is only a whis-per. Speaking helps bring what has been held inside into the open, and that is often where peace begins to lift. One thing matters here: clarity. If something comes to mind naturally, name it honestly and spe-cifically. If nothing comes to mind, or a section does not apply to you, simply move on.

This process works through honesty and clarity—not pressure.

If you already believe God is real and personal, speak this prayer to Him as written. If you are unsure, skeptical, or still sorting out what you believe, you do not need to manufacture belief. You can still speak honestly to God as best you know how and simply notice what happens.

How to Use This Prayer

This prayer is not meant to be rushed.

For many people, peace settles most fully when this prayer is spoken more than once—often over a few days. Not because peace is fragile—but because alignment often unfolds in layers, and time allows what needs to surface to do so naturally.

Consider taking a few quiet minutes each day for the next three days to speak this prayer out loud. This simply creates space for whatever you've been carrying to come into the open.

If three days feels like too much, start with one day. You don't need to intensify your focus or repeat words unnecessarily. Just be honest. Name what comes to mind. Then let it go.

If nothing new comes to mind on a particular day, that's fine. Don't go searching. This isn't about digging—it's about clarity.

Use the words as a guide, not a script. If a phrase doesn't fit your background, say it in language that feels natural to you and continue.

When you're ready, continue to the prayer below. I have provided instructions and insights in brackets.

❖ A Prayer for Peace To Return ❖

[Pray this out loud. It does not need to be loud— whispering is fine—but do speak it.]

God, I come to You as the source of truth, order, and peace. Even if I'm still finding my footing, I choose honesty here. I desire to be fully aligned with what is true, life-giving, and in agreement with Your design for life. I acknowledge that some things in me—and some things done to me—have disrupted my peace, and I no longer want to carry the tension that resulted.

I ask You now to bring to my mind anything that needs to be addressed—anything that needs to be named, released, forgiven, or brought back into alignment with Your design—whether it is clear to me now or simply present beneath the surface—so that peace can be restored.

If I'm unsure what I believe right now, I speak this honestly and simply: if You are real and present, please guide me into truth and release so peace can be restored. Only bring what I'm ready to face, at the pace that is wise for me.

Releasing Unforgiveness

[Unresolved unforgiveness can keep something stuck inside—like a low-grade strain that won't fully release and quietly interferes with peace.]

I acknowledge that holding onto unforgiveness has created strain in my inner world. I now choose to forgive and release the following people who come to mind. I name them honestly and specifically, one by one. *(Name them here)*

For each person I have named, I release all judgments I have held against them. I let go of every internal attachment formed through resentment, offense, or unresolved anger.

I also release every unhealthy emotional and spiritual connection with those people—any connection that may be interfering with my peace. I choose to carry only what is truly mine, and to let go of the rest.

Releasing Lingering Attachments from Sexual Relationships

[Sexual relationships create deep bonds. When those bonds are formed without lasting clarity or commitment, or when they end without real closure, they can leave lingering emotional and spiritual attachment that disrupts peace long after the relationship has ended. This includes sexual encounters or relationships that were casual, temporary, secretive, repeated without resolution, or ended without closure.]

I acknowledge that some of my sexual relationships were out of alignment with Your design for life and created attachments that never fully released. I no longer want to carry the negative effects of those relationships.

For each person who now comes to mind, I name them privately and specifically, as feels wise and safe. *(Name them here)*

I release all unhealthy emotional or spiritual connections with each person I have named. I choose to carry only what is truly mine, and to let go of the rest.

I choose wholeness, clarity, and peace.

Releasing Harmful Spiritual Involvement

[Some spiritual experiences or influences—whether intentional or not—can leave a person feeling unsettled, confused, or internally unstable over time. This is not about shame or fear. If this doesn't connect with your experience, simply continue.]

I acknowledge as misaligned with Your truth any unhealthy spiritual involvement that may have contributed to unrest or inner instability. I now name each activity that comes to mind, and anyone who influenced me toward it. *(Name any activity and person here)*

For each activity and person I named, I now release every unhealthy spiritual attachment formed through that involvement.

Bringing Remaining Areas into Alignment

I also acknowledge as misaligned with Your truth any other actions, attitudes, or emotional patterns that now come to mind that fall short of what is true and life-giving and have disrupted my peace. *(Name each one specifically.)*

I choose truth over hiding and alignment over tension.

Removing What Does Not Belong

[This is an important step. It is not about force, volume, or emotional intensity. It is about clarity and alignment. When something no longer has a right to remain, it must be addressed directly. This is how alignment is completed and peace is fully restored.]

Standing in the permission and authority of God, anything blocking my peace connected with what I have named is no longer allowed to remain and must leave.

I also speak directly to _____ *(name a burden that has been disrupting your peace, such as anxiety, fear, heaviness, or persistent pain).* You must leave now. *(Repeat for each burden.)*

Receiving Peace

And now, God, I ask You to restore what was disrupted and reestablish peace where tension once lived.

I receive Your peace now. I allow it to settle. I allow it to remain.

Amen.

[Take a deep breath, hold it for a moment, then slowly exhale and relax.]

❖ (complete) ❖

What to Expect Over the Next Few Days

As you repeat this prayer daily over the next several days, what you may notice can vary from person to person—and all of it can be normal.

Some people experience a clear sense of peace the first day. Others notice a subtle lightness, a quiet calm, or a release of pressure they didn't realize they were carrying. For some, the change is gentle and unfolds gradually as alignment deepens, rather than arriving all at once.

You may also notice moments where old thoughts, emotions, or reactions briefly resurface during these days. This does not mean the prayer failed. Often it simply means something that no longer needs to be held is passing through awareness.

If anything feels confusing or too intense, slow down and return to simple honesty, then rest.

If peace feels steady, allow it to remain without trying to protect or intensify it. If peace feels uneven, let that be okay as well.

Alignment responds to honesty—not vigilance.

For the next several days, the most helpful posture is simple: notice what feels different without trying to label it, rest instead of evaluating, and if something unsettles you, return briefly to honesty—and then move on.

You are not repeating this prayer because something failed.

Each day simply allows what is ready to surface to do so naturally.

Peace is not fragile. As alignment unfolds, it continues without being forced.

If you sense that peace has begun but has not fully settled, you can go deeper and learn more about this process at **ThePrayerOfFreedom.com**. Everything there is explained clearly and without pressure. There is no rush. Peace responds to readiness.

If you noticed a shift—peace, lightness, emotion, even tears—at any point during these days, then something real may have lifted.

If you didn't feel anything yet, that's okay too. Peace does not always announce itself immediately. Sometimes it settles quietly, without drawing attention to itself.

Either way, something may already be changing. What matters is not how dramatic it felt, but that alignment has begun moving in the right direction.

For many people, this prayer brings a meaningful and lasting return of peace. For others—especially when there are deeper layers of long-standing tension, trauma, or repeated patterns—there may be more to address.

That's why there is a deeper, step-by-step process available for those who sense that peace has begun to return but is still settling over time. If that's you, **ThePrayerOfFreedom.com** walks through that process carefully and thoroughly. It's especially for people who feel relief begin—but notice the same pattern keeps resurfacing. What changes is not effort, but depth: you move through the layers one by one, with clear guidance.

There is no rush.

Something has already begun to settle—and may continue to do so over the coming days.

— Chapter 9 —
Where Peace Leads

If you've reached this point, something meaningful has already begun.

For some people, peace arrives immediately—clear, noticeable, undeniable.

For others, it becomes apparent as the days unfold—often the next morning. You wake up calmer. Less braced. Your body feels lighter. Your thoughts feel quieter. Nothing dramatic happened overnight, yet something is different.

Both are signs that something real has shifted.

For many, that is enough.

Peace settles. Life steadies. The internal noise fades, and what once felt heavy no longer dominates daily life. When the underlying obstructions to peace are removed, peace begins to feel natural again.

And what was released does not need to be carried again.

That doesn't mean peace becomes automatic forever. A life of peace still invites living in alignment with how God designed life to work. But peace itself is no longer something you have to prop up or maintain by force.

For some, this shows up in familiar, specific

ways. Peace may settle inside you—yet certain parts of life remain unchanged.

Relationships may still feel fractured or tense, even when you're doing your part. Long-standing conflict with a spouse, a child, a parent, or another family member may continue with no clear reason and no clean way forward.

Emotional patterns—anxiety, heaviness, anger, insecurity—may ease for a moment, then quietly return as if they were only waiting.

Physical issues may improve, yet pain, fatigue, or limitation still returns in cycles without explanation.

Sometimes the clearest sign is not what you feel inside—but what still has a grip on you or on someone you love.

That doesn't mean anything went wrong.

Often it simply means that what you experienced was a first step of restoration rather than the entire process.

What you experienced here is not a technique. It is an introduction—a beginning that allowed peace to return. But when struggles have been long-standing or layered over many years, they sometimes need to be addressed step by step.

For some people, this first shift is enough. For others, it reveals that there may be more beneath the surface—things that were not wrong, just unresolved.

That is why a deeper, step-by-step process exists for those who sense there is more to address.

It is not a different path—it is simply a deeper continuation of the same pattern you encountered here.

There is no urgency. Peace responds to readiness—not pressure.

But before you consider any next step, it's important to understand where peace actually comes from.

Peace did not come from the prayer itself.

Peace came from what happened when truth was brought into the open.

Peace comes from alignment with truth—truth woven into the way life was designed to function, whether we recognize it immediately or only come to understand it over time.

For some people, that truth is first experienced as a sense of inner settling—the quiet that comes when what's unresolved is finally brought into the open. For others, it is understood more spiritually and personally. Either way, the pattern is the same: when truth is brought honestly into the open before God, what was strained begins to release.

For me, that truth is personal. I believe peace ultimately comes from a Person—God. Not as an idea, but as the living source of truth and love.

If faith language is natural for you, you may recognize something more here. If it isn't, you can simply stay with what you've already experienced—and let understanding unfold over time.

Either way, this remains true: peace isn't produced by words. It flows when truth is welcomed into the light.

If you're unsure what you believe about God, that doesn't invalidate what you just experienced. You don't have to resolve every question to remain open to what is true.

The warmth, lightness, or quiet calm you may have felt is not merely a sensation. It reflects the removal of what once blocked peace—and the return of what is life-giving and whole.

I believe you were brought to this book for a reason. I believe God wants peace in your life because He loves you, and He invites you toward peace without force or fear.

For me, this is not about religion. It is about relationship.

God is not distant or abstract. He is personal. He is your Creator. And like any loving Father, He desires to be known—not because He needs anything from you, but because He made you for connection with Him.

If this resonates with you, the next step is simple.

It is not another book. It is not joining something. It is not saying the "right" words.

It is simply speaking honestly.

You might say something as simple as:

God, I want to know You more. Please reveal Yourself to me clearly. Lead me toward the people, places, or resources that will help me grow in understanding and relationship with You.

That kind of prayer is no different than a child turning to a loving parent and saying, *I want to be closer to you.* And just as a loving parent responds with joy and openness, God responds the same way.

Peace was never meant to be the destination.

It becomes the doorway to something deeper.

If peace has begun to return and you sense there may be more to understand or address, you can learn more about the deeper, step-by-step continuation at **ThePrayerOfFreedom.com**—clearly, thoughtfully, and without pressure.

A Quiet Thought Before You Move On

As you've read, you may have found yourself thinking of someone you care about—a friend, family member, or colleague—who seems weighed down, restless, or quietly overwhelmed.

If this book has helped you experience greater calm or clarity, consider sharing it, not as a fix, but as an invitation—a simple way of saying, "This helped me."

If you'd like to make it easy, you can simply point them to **OutrageousPeace.com**.

Many people never find books like this because they don't know what to look for—or they don't yet realize peace is possible. When readers leave brief reviews on Amazon, it helps the book appear for people who are actively searching—often at just the right time.

If you feel inclined, consider leaving a short review. It's not about promotion—it's a simple way to help this invitation reach people who are looking for it.

And if writing reviews isn't your thing, the simplest option is still the same: share **OutrageousPeace.com** with someone who comes to mind, or post it quietly where your friends can see it.

— Chapter 10 —
About *The Prayer of Freedom*

*O*utrageous *Peace* is designed to help restore peace by removing what interferes with alignment. For many people, that shift is enough. Peace settles, clarity returns, and life begins to steady again.

For others, a sense of peace returns—but something still feels unsettled.

When that happens, it's rarely because the process failed. More often, it means peace was only partially restored because some of the deeper causes of disruption remain unaddressed.

Some struggles are layered. They don't resolve all at once—especially when they've been present for years or have touched multiple areas of life.

Peace may arrive—sometimes clearly, sometimes quietly—yet certain struggles continue resurfacing: anxiety that returns without warning; emotional heaviness that lifts briefly but comes back; patterns of depression, addiction, relational conflict, physical pain, or inner unrest that seem resistant to lasting change.

These patterns are not random. And they are not a sign of weakness or lack of sincerity.

They often point to deeper spiritual roots—places where something remained unresolved, even though peace began to return.

The Prayer of Freedom was created for those situations.

It is not a different approach—it is a deeper step.

It is a structured, step-by-step prayer process designed to address deeper spiritual issues that can continue disrupting peace when they remain unresolved.

This is especially true when struggles overlap—when emotional, relational, and physical issues show up together, or when freedom feels close but never quite complete.

Outrageous Peace focuses on restoring internal calm and stability.

The Prayer of Freedom continues that process by helping address deeper layers that may still remain unresolved. The goal is not intensity or emotional release, but lasting alignment—and freedom that holds.

This process is especially helpful for people who recognize experiences like these:

- peace returns, but the same problems keep resurfacing
- progress feels real, yet incomplete
- emotional, physical, or relational struggles seem connected beneath the surface

- freedom feels close, but never quite final

For many people, *Outrageous Peace* opens the door. *The Prayer of Freedom* simply helps them continue walking through it.

If that description feels familiar, **ThePrayerOf-Freedom.com** explains how this prayer process works, who it's designed for, and how to approach it thoughtfully at your own pace.

There is no urgency and no pressure. This is not a step you're required to take—only an option if you sense there is more to be resolved.

— Chapter 11 —
Helping Others
by Giving It Forward

By the time you reach this point, you may already be noticing something subtle but meaningful.

A little more ease.

A little more room inside.

A sense that peace may not be as fragile as you once believed.

When peace begins to settle, something else often rises alongside it—not as a duty, but as a quiet awareness of the people around you.

Friends.

Family.

Coworkers.

People already in your life who carry ongoing weight—stress that never fully lifts, anxiety that won't quiet, physical pain, emotional strain, or a general sense of unrest.

When someone comes to mind, you may feel a simple nudge to share what helped you. Not to fix anything. Not to persuade or explain. Simply to place the book in their hands and allow them to explore it in their own way, at their own pace.

Many people share this message quietly. Often, simply giving the book to someone is enough.

Over time, I've learned the simple value of being ready. Opportunities to help people rarely announce themselves ahead of time. A conversation opens. Someone shares what they're carrying. And having a book available in that moment can make all the difference.

So, I keep a few extra copies of *Outrageous Peace* on hand. Not as a plan or a program—just as a way of being ready when the moment comes.

And if you have a place where others already listen to you—social media, a small community, or a personal page—you might choose to share a brief, honest note about what you experienced. Not as a recommendation or pitch—just as a quiet invitation for someone who may be searching for peace.

One simple sentence is enough. And if you want to give people an easy place to begin, you can simply point them to **OutrageousPeace.com**.

There is no expectation here—only an invitation for those who feel stirred.

A Gentle Daily Reset

If you'd like a simple daily prayer to stay in peace, there's a short guided Daily Peace prayer waiting for you.

It's a quiet pause to breathe, release, and realign.

Scan the code below or visit: OutrageousPeace.com/DailyPeace

RESOURCES

Sharing Copies with Others

If you wish to keep extra copies of *Outrageous Peace* on hand to share with others, discounted volume options are available at **OutrageousPeace.com**.

The Prayer of Freedom

If you want to go deeper, *The Prayer of Freedom* provides a focused, step-by-step process that applies the framework introduced in *Outrageous Peace* in a practical, hands-on way.

Learn more at **ThePrayerOfFreedom.com**.

This work is supported by Get Radical Faith Ministries, a nonprofit organization dedicated to helping people experience lasting peace and freedom.

THE PRAYER
OF FREEDOM

The Prayer of Freedom is a practical, step-by-step guide that applies the spiritual framework introduced in *Outrageous Peace* in a focused, hands-on way. Written for readers who want to go deeper, it explains how these spiritual principles operate at the root level of personal struggle—addressing chronic emotional pressure, recurring patterns, and unresolved struggles that don't respond to surface-level solutions. It is designed as an active process for those ready to move beyond understanding peace and begin restoring it.

NUGGETS
OF FAITH

Nuggets of Faith is a devotional collection of insights and revelations God taught Beatty Carmichael over five-and-a-half years of personal study. These entries were first written as personal notes he received from God and later compiled, at God's prompting, into a devotional resource to be shared with others. Written for readers who desire more than surface-level familiarity with Scripture, this book serves as a daily guide for deepening understanding of God's truth and applying it with clarity and confidence.

ABOUT THE AUTHOR

Beatty Carmichael is a Bible teacher, spiritual guide, and founder of Get Radical Faith Ministries. His work focuses on helping people experience calm, clarity, and freedom by understanding the spiritual order that quietly shapes the inner life.

For decades, Beatty has taught biblical truth and spiritual principles that lead to real-world transformation—not through pressure or performance, but through alignment with what is true and life-giving. What began as personal ministry evolved into a clear, repeatable process that has helped thousands experience meaningful and lasting shifts in peace, stability, and freedom.

As the leader of Get Radical Faith Ministries, Beatty is committed to helping people move beyond surface-level faith into a lived experience of spiritual maturity and wholeness. Guided by Luke 6:40—"a disciple is not above the teacher, but when fully trained will become like the teacher"—his work emphasizes practical application, personal growth, and daily alignment with truth.

Beatty lives in Birmingham, Alabama, with his wife, Peggie. They have three grown children and share a passion for helping others experience the peace and freedom they were meant to live with.

To learn more about his teachings, request a

speaking engagement, or explore additional resources, visit **BeattyCarmichael.com.**